# BERRIES

MARKS &
SPENCER

# BERRIES

COOKERY CONSULTANT
PAMELA GWYTHER

Marks and Spencer p.l.c.
PO Box 3339
Chester CH99 9QS
www.marksandspencer.com

T40/8283/0212D

ISBN: 1-84461-463-8

Printed in China

Produced by The Bridgewater Book Company Ltd
Photographer: David Jordan
Home economist: Jacqueline Bellefontaine

Notes for the Reader

This book uses both metric and imperial measurements. Follow the
same units of measurement throughout; do not mix metric and
imperial. All spoon measurements are level: teaspoons are assumed
to be 5 ml, and tablespoons are assumed to be 15 ml. Unless
otherwise stated, milk is assumed to be full fat, eggs and individual
vegetables such as potatoes are medium and pepper is freshly
ground black pepper. Recipes using raw or very lightly cooked
eggs should be avoided by infants, the elderly, pregnant women,
convalescents and anyone suffering from an illness. The times given
are an approximate guide only. Preparation times differ according
to the techniques used by different people and the cooking times
may also vary from those given. Optional ingredients, variations or
serving suggestions have not been included in the calculations.

**Picture acknowledgments**
The Bridgewater Book Company would like to thank the following for
permission to reproduce copyright material: Corbis Images, pages 8 & 48;
Altrendo/Getty Images, pages 6 & 72; and FoodPix/Getty Images, endpapers.

# CONTENTS

Berries contain such a wide variety of nutrients that they have gained the status of 'superfood'. Red berries, for example, are rich in vitamin C, while blueberries are good for detoxing the body and maintaining body functions such as balance and coordination, circulation and eyesight. Blackberries are high in fibre, folic acid and vitamin C, and blackcurrants have valuable antibacterial qualities.

The most common berries are strawberries, raspberries and blackberries. Blueberries are becoming increasingly popular, and are reputed to guard against urinary tract infections. Cranberries are delicious in cranberry sauce, pies and desserts, while green gooseberries are excellent for pies and crumbles, and make a sharp, piquant sauce for oily fish and rich foods. Juniper berries, famous for flavouring gin, lend their pungent qualities to savoury dishes, while tayberries, mulberries, loganberries,

# INTRODUCTION

boysenberries and bilberries are becoming more easily available.

Although not strictly 'berries', redcurrants and blackcurrants are included in this book, since they are used in similar ways to true berries.

To enjoy berries at their best, use them fresh and when in season. Most berries are acceptable frozen when cooked in a recipe, apart from strawberries, which do not freeze well.

We all know how delicious berries are, eaten fresh with cream or ice cream, or baked in pies and used in other fruit-based desserts, but here is the perfect opportunity to widen your perspective on berries. You will see in this collection of innovative recipes how effortlessly they add a whole new dimension to a wide variety of savoury dishes to give an exciting taste sensation. And as an extra bonus, they contribute natural, vibrant colour.

Start by dispelling your preconceptions with the delicious Strawberry Soup, which acts as a wonderful palate sharpener and is a much lighter alternative first course to a traditional soup. Berries are also great in salads, as you will soon

# PART ONE
# THE MAIN EVENT

discover, and instantly enhance them with their sun-ripened flavour – ideal for enjoying alfresco on a hot day. You will also see how they can transform simple grilled or pan-fried meat and poultry with a tangy, piquant berry sauce or relish, which is also a simple, smart way of adding to your five-a-day fruit and vegetable target. The sharpness of berries also has the ability to cut through the fattiness of some foods, such as duck, to improve their flavour and aid digestion.

All these recipes demonstrate how berries can be used to make tastier, healthier meals, and give an imaginative, contemporary twist to classic dishes.

# STRAWBERRY SOUP

**SERVES 6**

900 g/2 lb fresh
strawberries

200 ml/7 fl oz cranberry
juice

200 ml/7 fl oz dry white
wine or apple juice

175 g/6 oz créme fraîche

fresh mint sprigs,
to garnish

Pick over the strawberries and hull. Reserve
175 g/6 oz. Put the remainder of the fruit in
a large saucepan with the cranberry juice,
and cook over a medium heat until the fruit
is softened.

Leave to cool slightly, then transfer the fruit
and juice to a blender or food processor and
process until smooth.

Add the wine, process briefly to combine,
then pour into a jug. Cover with clingfilm and
chill in the refrigerator.

Meanwhile, slice the reserved strawberries.

Pour the soup into 6 bowls and float the
sliced strawberries on top. Top with a spoonful
of créme fraîche and garnish with mint sprigs.
Serve immediately.

IF YOU PREFER, YOU CAN PROCESS
THE UNCOOKED STRAWBERRIES IN
A BLENDER OR FOOD PROCESSOR
INSTEAD OF COOKING THEM,
WHICH GIVES A SHARPER FLAVOUR.

# SALMON FISHCAKES WITH GOOSEBERRY SAUCE

**SERVES 6**

450 g/1 lb salmon fillets, skinned

450 g/1 lb potatoes, peeled, boiled and mashed

2 tbsp chopped fresh parsley

grated rind of 1 lemon

2 tbsp double cream

1 tbsp plain flour

1 egg, beaten

115 g/4 oz wholemeal breadcrumbs, made from one-day-old bread

4 tbsp vegetable oil, for shallow-frying

salt and pepper

fresh salad, to serve

*Gooseberry sauce*

225 g/8 oz fresh gooseberries

25 g/1 oz butter, softened

1–2 tbsp sugar, to taste

pinch of ground ginger (optional)

Put the fish in a large saucepan and just cover with water. Bring to the boil over a medium heat, then reduce the heat, cover and simmer gently for 5 minutes until cooked.

Remove from the heat. Using a slotted spoon, lift the fish out on to a plate. When cool enough to handle, flake the fish roughly into bite-sized pieces, ensuring that there are no stray bones.

Mix the mashed potatoes with the fish, parsley, lemon rind and cream. Season well with salt and pepper and shape into 6 round cakes.

Put the flour, beaten egg and breadcrumbs into 3 separate shallow bowls. Dust the fishcakes with flour, dip them into the beaten egg and coat thoroughly in the breadcrumbs. Transfer to a baking sheet, cover with clingfilm and chill in the refrigerator for at least 30 minutes.

Meanwhile, make the sauce. Top and tail the gooseberries and put in a saucepan with a little cold water. Cook over a low heat until the fruit is softened to a pulp. Remove from the heat and beat well with a wooden spoon until smooth, or transfer to a blender or food processor and process until smooth. Beat in the butter, and sugar to taste (gooseberries vary in their acidity). Add the ginger, if using, and transfer to a small serving bowl.

Heat the oil in a frying pan over a medium heat. Fry the fishcakes for 5 minutes on each side, turning them carefully with a palette knife or fish slice. Remove from the frying pan and drain on kitchen paper.

Serve the fishcakes with the sauce and accompanied by a fresh salad.

TRY SMOKED TROUT OR SMOKED MACKEREL INSTEAD OF THE SALMON FILLETS – SMOKED FISH DOES NOT NEED TO BE PRECOOKED.

# RASPBERRY AND FETA SALAD
## WITH COUSCOUS

**SERVES 6**

350 g/12 oz couscous

600 ml/1 pint boiling
chicken stock or
vegetable stock

350 g/12 oz fresh
raspberries

small bunch of fresh basil

225 g/8 oz feta cheese,
cubed or crumbled

2 courgettes, thinly sliced

4 spring onions, trimmed
and diagonally sliced

55 g/2 oz pine kernels,
toasted

grated rind of 1 lemon

*Dressing*

1 tbsp white wine vinegar

1 tbsp balsamic vinegar

4 tbsp extra-virgin
olive oil

juice of 1 lemon

salt and pepper

INSTEAD OF COUSCOUS, YOU
COULD USE CRACKED WHEAT
FOR A CRUNCHIER SALAD.

Put the couscous in a large, heatproof bowl and
pour over the stock. Stir well, cover and leave to
soak until all the stock has been absorbed.

Pick over the raspberries, discarding any that
are overripe. Shred the basil leaves.

Transfer the couscous to a large serving bowl
and stir well to break up any lumps. Add the
cheese, vegetables, raspberries and pine kernels.
Stir in the basil and lemon rind and gently toss
all the ingredients together.

Put all the dressing ingredients in a screw-top
jar, with salt and pepper to taste, screw on the
lid and shake until well blended. Pour over the
salad and serve.

# SMOKED CHICKEN AND CRANBERRY SALAD

**SERVES 4**

1 smoked chicken, weighing 1.3 kg/3 lb

115 g/4 oz dried cranberries

2 tbsp apple juice or water

200 g/7 oz sugar snap peas

2 ripe avocados

juice of 1/2 lemon

4 lettuce hearts

1 bunch of watercress, trimmed

55 g/2 oz rocket

55 g/2 oz walnuts, chopped, to garnish (optional)

*Dressing*

2 tbsp olive oil

1 tbsp walnut oil

2 tbsp lemon juice

1 tbsp chopped fresh mixed herbs, such as parsley and lemon thyme

salt and pepper

DRIED CHERRIES OR OTHER DRIED FRUIT CAN BE USED INSTEAD OF THE CRANBERRIES.

Carve the chicken carefully, slicing the white meat. Divide the legs into thighs and drumsticks and trim the wings. Cover with clingfilm and refrigerate.

Put the cranberries in a bowl. Stir in the apple juice, cover with clingfilm and leave to soak for 30 minutes.

Meanwhile, blanch the sugar snap peas, refresh under cold running water and drain.

Peel, stone and slice the avocados, then toss in the lemon juice to prevent browning.

Separate the lettuce hearts and arrange on a large serving platter with the avocados, sugar snap peas, watercress, rocket and the chicken.

Put all the dressing ingredients, with salt and pepper to taste, in a screw-top jar, screw on the lid and shake until well blended.

Drain the cranberries and mix them with the dressing, then pour over the salad.

Serve immediately, scattered with walnuts if you are using them.

# SKEWERED CHICKEN WITH BRAMBLE SAUCE

**SERVES 4**

4 skinless, boneless
chicken breasts or
8 thighs

4 tbsp dry white wine
or cider

2 tbsp chopped fresh
rosemary

1/4 tsp freshly grated
nutmeg

pepper

fresh rosemary sprigs,
to garnish

green salad, to serve

*Bramble sauce*

200 g/7 oz blackberries,
plus extra to garnish

1 tbsp cider vinegar

2 tbsp redcurrant jelly

Using a sharp knife, cut the chicken into 2.5-cm/1-inch pieces and put in a bowl. Sprinkle over the wine and chopped rosemary and season well with pepper. Cover and leave to marinate in the refrigerator for at least an hour.

Preheat the grill to medium-high. Drain the chicken, reserving the marinade, and thread the meat on to 8 metal skewers, or wooden skewers presoaked in cold water for 30 minutes.

Cook the chicken under the grill, turning the scewers occasionally, for 8–10 minutes until golden brown, tender and cooked through.

Meanwhile, to make the sauce, put the reserved marinade in a saucepan with the blackberries and cook over a low heat until the fruit is softened. Using the back of a wooden spoon, press the mixture through a nylon sieve into a bowl to form a purée.

Return the blackberry purée to the saucepan, add the vinegar and redcurrant jelly and bring to the boil. Boil, uncovered, until the sauce is reduced by about one-third.

Spoon a little sauce onto each plate and put two chicken skewers on top. Sprinkle with the nutmeg and serve hot, garnished with rosemary sprigs and blackberries, accompanied by a green salad.

THIS AUTUMNAL RECIPE CAN BE MADE WITH FRESHLY PICKED WILD BLACKBERRIES FROM THE HEDGEROW IF YOU ARE LUCKY ENOUGH TO HAVE A GOOD LOCAL SUPPLY. IF YOU HAVE TO USE CANNED FRUIT, OMIT THE REDCURRANT JELLY.

# DUCK WITH BERRY SAUCE

**SERVES 4**

450 g/1 lb boneless
duck breasts

2 tbsp raspberry vinegar

2 tbsp brandy

1 tbsp clear honey

1 tsp sunflower oil,
for brushing

salt and pepper

2 kiwi fruit, peeled and
thinly sliced to serve

*Berry sauce*

225 g/8 oz raspberries,
thawed if frozen

300 ml/10 fl oz rosé wine

2 tsp cornflour, blended
with 4 tsp cold water

Skin the duck breasts and discard any excess fat.
Using a sharp knife, score the flesh of each
duck breast in diagonal lines and pound it with
a covered rolling pin or meat mallet until it is
2 cm/³/4 inch thick.

Put the duck breasts in a shallow, non-metallic
dish. Mix the vinegar, brandy and honey together
in a small bowl and spoon it over the duck.
Cover with clingfilm and leave to marinate in the
refrigerator for about an hour.

Preheat the grill to medium. Drain the duck,
reserving the marinade, and put on the grill
rack. Season to taste with salt and pepper and
brush with a little oil. Cook under the grill for
10 minutes, then turn over, season to taste with
salt and pepper and brush with oil again. Cook
for a further 8–10 minutes until the meat is
tender and cooked through.

Meanwhile, to make the sauce, reserve about
55 g/2 oz of the raspberries and put the
remainder in a saucepan. Add the reserved
marinade and the wine. Bring to the boil, then
reduce the heat and simmer for 5 minutes, or
until slightly reduced. Using the back of a
wooden spoon, press the mixture through a
nylon sieve into a bowl to form a purée.

Return the purée to the saucepan and stir in
the cornflour paste. Cook, stirring constantly,
until thickened. Add the reserved raspberries
and season to taste with salt and pepper.

Thinly slice the duck breast and serve with
slices of kiwi fruit on warmed serving plates with
the sauce spooned over.

IF YOU CAN'T FIND RASPBERRY VINEGAR,
USE RED WINE VINEGAR INSTEAD.

# GRILLED LAMB CHOPS WITH REDCURRANT SAUCE

**SERVES 4**

4 thick gigot of lamb chops, about 200–250 g/7–9 oz each and 2.5 cm/1 inch thick

*Marinade*

2 garlic cloves, sliced

4 fresh rosemary sprigs, plus extra to garnish

2 tbsp olive oil

125 ml/4 fl oz red wine

salt and pepper

*Redcurrant sauce*

225 g/8 oz fresh redcurrants or cranberries, plus extra to garnish

40 g/1½ oz caster sugar

1 tbsp balsamic vinegar

175 ml/6 fl oz red wine

pinch of ground cinnamon

grated rind of 1 orange

*To serve*

new potatoes tossed in chopped fresh mint

green vegetables

Arrange the lamb chops in a single layer in a shallow, non-metallic dish. Scatter over the garlic and rosemary. Pour over the oil and wine and season well with salt and pepper. Cover with clingfilm and leave to marinate in the refrigerator for at least 2 hours, or preferably overnight.

Meanwhile, make the sauce. Strip the redcurrants from their stalks using the prongs of a fork and put in a small saucepan with the sugar, vinegar and wine over a low heat. Bring slowly to a simmer, then add the cinnamon and orange rind. Cook gently until the redcurrants are softened and the sauce is a

good consistency. Beat with a wooden spoon to make a coarse purée. Using the back of a wooden spoon, press the mixture through a nylon sieve into a bowl to remove the seeds.

When you are ready to cook the chops, preheat the grill to high. Remove the chops from the marinade, discarding any slices of garlic and rosemary sprigs. Cook the chops under the grill for 2–3 minutes on one side, depending on how you like your lamb cooked. Turn the chops over and cook until done to taste.

Serve immediately with the sauce, new potatoes and green vegetables and garnished with rosemary sprigs and redcurrants.

THE REDCURRANT SAUCE CAN BE MADE IN ADVANCE AND REHEATED WHEN NEEDED. YOU CAN ALSO BARBECUE THE LAMB CHOPS.

# VEAL ESCALOPES WITH BLACKBERRY AND APPLE RELISH

**SERVES 4**

4 veal escalopes, about 175 g/6 oz each

25 g/1 oz butter

1 tbsp sunflower or vegetable oil

2 shallots, finely chopped

1 cooking apple, peeled, cored and finely chopped

25 g/1 oz demerara sugar

$^1/_2$ tsp ground ginger

2 tbsp balsamic vinegar

150 g/5$^1/_2$ oz fresh blackberries

salt and pepper

fresh green salad, to serve

Preheat the oven to 150°C/300°F/Gas Mark 2. Put the escalopes between 2 sheets of clingfilm and beat with a rolling pin or a meat mallet until thin.

Heat the butter in a frying pan over a high heat and cook the escalopes for 2–3 minutes on each side until lightly browned. You may need to do this in 2 batches if the escalopes are large. Remove from the frying pan, season well with salt and pepper and keep warm in the preheated oven.

Heat the oil in the frying pan and cook the shallots until softened. Add the apple, sugar, ginger and vinegar to the frying pan, stir well and cook for 3–4 minutes until the apple is softened. Add the blackberries and cook for a further 2–3 minutes until the relish is well reduced and all the fruit is softened. Season to taste with salt and pepper.

Put the escalopes onto warmed serving plates and serve with a fresh green salad and the relish alongside.

YOU COULD USE VEAL OR PORK CHOPS IN THIS RECIPE INSTEAD OF ESCALOPES – THEY WOULD NEED TO BE COOKED FOR LONGER BECAUSE THEY ARE THICKER.

# PORK WITH FENNEL AND JUNIPER BERRIES

**SERVES 4**

1/2 fennel bulb

1 tbsp juniper berries

2 tbsp olive oil

finely grated rind and juice of 1 orange

4 pork chops, about 150 g/5 1/2 oz each

*To serve*

crisp salad

fresh bread

JUNIPER BERRIES ARE OFTEN ADDED TO ITALIAN MEAT DISHES FOR A DELICATE CITRUS FLAVOUR. THEY CAN BE BOUGHT DRIED FROM HEALTH FOOD SHOPS AND LARGE SUPERMARKETS.

Trim and finely chop the fennel bulb, discarding the green parts.

Crush the juniper berries in a mortar with a pestle. Mix with the fennel, oil and orange rind in a bowl.

Using a sharp knife, score the flesh of each pork chop in diagonal lines. Put the chops in a roasting tin or ovenproof dish. Spoon the fennel and juniper berry mixture over the top. Pour over the orange juice, cover with clingfilm and leave to marinate in the refrigerator for about 2 hours.

Preheat the grill to medium. Cook the pork chops under the grill, turning occasionally, for 10–15 minutes, depending on the thickness of the meat, or until the meat is tender and cooked through.

Transfer the chops to serving plates and serve with a crisp salad and plenty of fresh bread to mop up the cooking juices.

# SAUSAGES WITH CRANBERRY AND RED ONION MARMALADE

**SERVES 4**

8 good-quality sausages

1 tbsp sunflower or
vegetable oil

*Marmalade*

3 tbsp olive oil

400 g/14 oz red onions,
halved and finely sliced

150 ml/5 fl oz red wine

2 tbsp balsamic vinegar

55 g/2 oz dark muscovado
sugar

225 g/8 oz fresh
cranberries

*To serve*

mashed potato

green vegeables

Preheat the oven to 200°C/400°F/Gas Mark 6. Put the sausages in a small roasting tin and pour over the sunflower oil. Roll the sausages in the oil until well coated.

Roast the sausages in the preheated oven for 25–30 minutes. Alternatively, cook the sausages in a frying pan over a low heat, turning occasionally, until well browned and sticky.

Meanwhile, heat the olive oil in a wide saucepan and cook the onions over a medium heat, stirring frequently to prevent them sticking to the saucepan, for 10–15 minutes until very soft and browned. Add the wine, vinegar and sugar and stir until the sugar has dissolved. Cook for a further 10 minutes until the liquid is reduced and the onions are sticky.

Add the cranberries and stir well. Cook for 4–5 minutes until the cranberries have burst and the mixture is the consistency of chutney. Remove the marmalade from the heat and serve with the sausages, mashed potato and green vegetables.

THE MARMALADE CAN BE STORED IN AN AIRTIGHT CONTAINER IN THE REFRIGERATOR FOR UP TO 1 WEEK AND CAN BE SERVED WARM OR COLD WITH SALADS AND COLD CUTS. IT IS ALSO PERFECT FOR SERVING WITH ROAST TURKEY FOR CHRISTMAS LUNCH.

In this chapter, we see how berries can be used to create delicious, healthful breakfasts and snacks, as well as lighter bites for in between that fit today's busy lifestyles. But let's not forget that they can also be at the heart of some truly indulgent dishes too.

Berries make the perfect, nutritious way to start the day, either in a classic cereal or in a modern-style smoothie. Quick and easy to prepare, the drinks also make a refreshing snack at any time of the day and are a far healthier alternative to processed snacks such as biscuits and crisps. But when it's the weekend and you feel in need of something a little more luxurious,

# PART TWO
# A LIGHT MOMENT

choose from Blueberry Pancakes drizzled with warm maple syrup and Spiced French Toast with Seasonal Berries for a late breakfast or brunch.

For teatime, why not try a fresh, healthful take on that perennial favourite of scones, jam and cream: Banana Bread with Strawberry Compote and Mascarpone, flavoured with warm, sweet spices. In fact, this is substantial enough to be served as a brunch or to eat as a between-meal snack. But if it's a traditional taste of teatime that you crave, you can't beat real home-made jam, just like grandma used to make. Even if you have time to make only one batch of four or five jars, it will be a real treat for you and your family.

# BILBERRY
# BIRCHER MUESLI

**SERVES 2**

100 g/3 1/2 oz jumbo oats

200 ml/7 fl oz apple juice

1 red apple, cored

1 tbsp lemon juice

25 g/1 oz toasted
hazelnuts, chopped

1/2 tsp ground cinnamon

100 ml/3 1/2 fl oz natural
bio yogurt

2 tbsp runny honey
(optional)

70 g/2 1/2 oz fresh
bilberries or blueberries

Put the oats and apple juice in a bowl, cover with clingfilm and leave to soak in the refrigerator for an hour. You can do this the night before.

Grate or chop the apple and mix with the lemon juice to prevent browning.

Add the apple, hazelnuts and cinnamon to the oat mixture and mix well.

Spoon the mixture into serving bowls and top with the yogurt. Drizzle over the honey, if using. Spoon the bilberries over the muesli and serve.

IF BILBERRIES OR BLUEBERRIES ARE UNAVAILABLE, SUBSTITUTE ANY OTHER FRESH BERRIES. ADD A SLICED BANANA FOR A MORE SUBSTANTIAL SNACK.

# BLUEBERRY
## PANCAKES

**MAKES 10–12**

140 g/5 oz plain flour

2 tbsp caster sugar

2 tbsp baking powder

1/2 tsp salt

225 ml/8 fl oz buttermilk

3 tbsp butter, melted

1 large egg

140 g/5 oz fresh
blueberries

sunflower or corn oil,
for oiling

*To serve*

butter

warm maple syrup

Preheat the oven to 140°C/275°F/Gas Mark 1.
Sieve the flour, sugar, baking powder and salt
together into a large bowl and make a well in
the centre.

Beat the buttermilk, butter and egg together
in a separate small bowl, then pour the mixture
into the well in the dry ingredients. Beat the dry
ingredients into the liquid, gradually drawing
them in from the side, until a smooth batter is
formed. Gently stir in the blueberries.

Heat a large frying pan over a medium-high
heat until a splash of water dances on the
surface. Using a pastry brush or crumpled piece
of kitchen paper, oil the base of the frying pan.

Drop about 4 tablespoons of batter
separately into the frying pan and spread each
out into a 10-cm/4-inch round. Continue adding
as many pancakes as will fit in your frying pan.
Cook until small bubbles appear on the surface,
then flip over with a spatula or palette knife and
cook the pancakes on the other side for a further
1–2 minutes until the bases are golden brown.

Transfer the pancakes to a warmed plate and
keep warm in the preheated oven while you
cook the remaining batter, lightly oiling the frying
pan as before. Make a stack of the pancakes with
baking paper in between each pancake.

Serve with a knob of butter on top of
each pancake and warm maple syrup for
pouring over.

# SPICED FRENCH TOAST WITH SEASONAL BERRIES

**SERVES 4**

4 eggs, plus I extra egg
white

¹/₄ tsp ground cinnamon

¹/₄ tsp mixed spice

4 slices thick white bread

I tbsp butter, melted

fresh mint sprigs,
to decorate

*Berries*

85 g/3 oz caster sugar

50 ml/2 fl oz freshly
squeezed orange juice

300 g/10¹/₂ oz mixed fresh
seasonal berries, such as
strawberries, raspberries
and blueberries, picked
over and hulled

Preheat the oven to 220°C/425°F/Gas Mark 7.
Put the eggs and egg white in a large, shallow
bowl or dish and whisk together with a fork.
Add the cinnamon and mixed spice and whisk
until combined.

To prepare the berries, put the sugar and
orange juice in a saucepan and bring to the boil
over a low heat, stirring until the sugar has
dissolved. Add the berries, remove from the heat
and leave to cool for 10 minutes.

Meanwhile, soak the bread slices in the egg
mixture for about I minute on each side. Brush
a large baking sheet with the melted butter and
place the bread slices on the sheet. Bake in the
preheated oven for 5–7 minutes, or until lightly
browned. Turn the slices over and bake for a
further 2–3 minutes. Serve the berries spooned
over the toast and decorated with mint sprigs.

THIS OVEN-BAKED METHOD
OF MAKING FRENCH TOAST
USES MUCH LESS FAT THAN
THE SHALLOW-FRIED VERSION
AND MAKES IT EASY TO
PRODUCE LARGER QUANTITIES.

# STRAWBERRY JAM

**MAKES 5 x 450-G/1-LB JARS**

1.6 kg/3 lb 8 oz fresh strawberries

3 tbsp lemon juice

1.3 kg/3 lb granulated or preserving sugar

Preheat the oven to 180°C/350°F/Gas Mark 4. Sterilize five 450-g/1-lb jam jars with screw-top lids.

Pick over the strawberries, discarding any that are overripe, and hull. Put the fruit in a large saucepan with the lemon juice and heat over a low heat until some of the fruit juices begin to run. Continue to simmer gently for 10–15 minutes until softened.

Add the sugar and stir until it has dissolved. Increase the heat and boil rapidly for 2–3 minutes until setting point is reached. Test the mixture with a sugar thermometer – it should read 105°C/221°F for a good setting point. Alternatively, drop a teaspoonful of jam on to a cold saucer, place it in the refrigerator to cool it, and then push it with your finger. If it forms a wrinkled skin, it is ready. If not, boil for a further minute and repeat.

Remove the saucepan from the heat and leave to cool for 15–20 minutes, to prevent the fruit rising in the jar. Skim if necessary.

Meanwhile, warm the jam jars in the preheated oven. Remove and fill carefully with the jam, using a ladle and a jam funnel. Top with waxed discs, waxed-side down, and screw on the lids tightly. Wipe the jars clean and leave to cool. Label and date to avoid confusion later.

Store in a cool, dry place. Once opened, it is advisable to keep the jar in the refrigerator.

STRAWBERRIES HAVE LITTLE PECTIN IN THEM TO HELP SET THE JAM, SO IT IS IMPORTANT TO ADD THE LEMON JUICE.

# QUICK RASPBERRY JAM

**MAKES 4 x 450-G/1-LB JARS**

1.3 kg/3 lb granulated or preserving sugar

1 kg/2 lb 4 oz fresh raspberries

Preheat the oven to 160°C/325°F/Gas Mark 3. Sterilize four 450-g/1-lb jam jars with screw-top lids.

Put the sugar in a large, heatproof bowl and warm in the preheated oven.

Meanwhile, pick over the raspberries, discarding any that are overripe. Put the fruit in a large saucepan and heat over a low heat until some of the fruit juices begin to run. Simmer gently for 2–3 minutes until softened.

Add the warmed sugar and stir until it has dissolved. Increase the oven temperature to 180°C/350°F/Gas Mark 4.

Increase the heat and boil the jam rapidly for 2–3 minutes. Remove from the heat and leave to cool for 2 minutes. Skim if necessary.

Meanwhile, warm the jam jars in the oven. Remove and fill carefully with the jam, using a ladle and a jam funnel. Top with waxed discs, waxed-side down, and screw on the lids tightly. Wipe the jars clean and leave to cool. Label and date to avoid confusion later.

Store in a cool, dry place. Once opened, it is advisable to keep the jar in the refrigerator. This jam does not have a very firm set, but it does have a delicious flavour.

IF THE RASPBERRIES HAVE A LOT OF SEEDS, YOU CAN SIEVE SOME OF THE JAM TO REDUCE THE AMOUNT.

# BANANA BREAD WITH STRAWBERRY COMPOTE AND MASCARPONE

**SERVES 8**

125 g/4¹/₂ oz butter, softened, plus extra for greasing

100 g/3¹/₂ oz caster sugar

55 g/2 oz soft brown sugar

3 eggs

1 tsp vanilla extract

3 large, ripe bananas

250 g/9 oz self-raising flour

1 tsp freshly grated nutmeg

1 tsp ground cinnamon

icing sugar, sifted, for dusting (optional)

mascarpone cheese or natural yogurt, to serve

*Strawberry compote*

85 g/3 oz soft brown sugar

juice of 2 oranges

grated rind of 1 orange

1 cinnamon stick

400 g/14 oz fresh strawberries, hulled and thickly sliced

Preheat the oven to 180°C/350°F/Gas Mark 4. Grease a 23 x 11-cm/9 x 4¹/₄-inch loaf tin and line the base with nonstick baking paper.

Put the butter and sugars in a bowl and beat together until light and fluffy. Mix in the eggs, one at a time, then mix in the vanilla extract. Peel the bananas and mash roughly with the back of a fork. Stir gently into the butter mixture, then add the flour, nutmeg and cinnamon, stirring until just combined.

Pour the mixture into the prepared tin and bake in the preheated oven for 1¹/₄ hours, or until a skewer inserted into the centre comes out clean. Leave in the tin for 5 minutes before turning out on to a wire rack to cool.

To make the compote, put the sugar, orange juice and rind and cinnamon stick in a saucepan and bring to the boil. Add the strawberries and return to the boil. Remove from the heat, pour into a clean heatproof bowl and leave to cool. Remove the cinnamon stick. Serve slices of the banana bread with a dollop of mascarpone cheese or yogurt and spoon over the warm or cold compote. Dust with sifted icing sugar if desired.

THE BREAD CAN BE STORED IN THE FREEZER FOR UP TO THREE MONTHS. THAW OVERNIGHT IN THE REFRIGERATOR BEFORE SERVING. IT CAN ALSO BE ICED FOR A DELICIOUS TEATIME TREAT.

# SUMMER AND CITRUS FRUIT PUNCH

**SERVES 2**

4 tbsp orange juice

I tbsp lime juice

100 ml/3$^1$/$_2$ fl oz sparkling water

4 ice cubes

350 g/12 oz frozen summer berries, such as blueberries, raspberries, blackberries and strawberries

whole strawberries, raspberries, blackcurrants and blackberries on cocktail sticks, to decorate

Pour the orange juice, lime juice and sparkling water into a blender or food processor and gently process until combined.

Put the ice cubes between 2 clean cloths and crush with a rolling pin. Add to the blender with the frozen berries and process until a slushy consistency has been reached.

Pour the mixture into glasses, decorate with whole strawberries, raspberries, blackcurrants and blackberries on cocktail sticks and serve.

To give this punch a fragrant twist, substitute dry ginger ale for the sparkling water. For an alcoholic version, replace the sparkling water with sparkling white wine.

# STRAWBERRY AND PEACH SMOOTHIE

**SERVES 2**

175 ml/6 fl oz milk

225 g/8 oz canned peach slices, drained

2 fresh apricots, chopped

400 g/14 oz fresh strawberries

2 bananas, sliced and frozen

Pour the milk into a blender or food processor. Add the peach slices and gently process until combined. Add the apricots and gently process again until combined.

Pick over the strawberries and hull, reserving 1 to decorate. Add the strawberries and frozen banana slices and process until smooth. Pour the mixture into glasses. Slice the reserved strawberry and use to decorate the glasses. Serve immediately.

YOU CAN EASILY VARY THIS RECIPE TO MAKE DIFFERENT FLAVOURED SMOOTHIES. USE RASPBERRIES OR BLUEBERRIES IN PLACE OF THE STRAWBERRIES, OR A SMALL PEELED, STONED MANGO INSTEAD OF THE APRICOTS. OR TRY REPLACING THE BANANAS WITH A COUPLE OF SCOOPS OF VANILLA OR EVEN CHOCOLATE ICE CREAM.

We are going back to traditional cooking in this chapter, and the art of making cakes and other baked treats and desserts. Home baking is not just rewarding in creating memorable food for family and friends, but is in itself highly therapeutic. Mixing a cake by hand in the calm and warmth of the kitchen can provide a soothing retreat from the hurly burly of our busy lives. And the results of your labours will always be welcomed by the recipients – children in particular. They might even help and get to lick the mixing bowl!

Here we have some long-established desserts, such as crumble and cobbler, elevated out of the everyday with the addition of succulent berries and currants. Other firm family favourites include muffins, shortcake and cheesecake, made sumptuous with blueberries, strawberries and gooseberries. But you don't have to wait for dessert to enjoy fruit-filled delights. Those old

# PART THREE
# TEATIME TREATS

faithful lunch box or picnic companions, brownies and flapjacks, are enriched here with luscious loganberries and chewy dried cranberries and blueberries, and will provide an energy-boosting snack when you're on the move, or a delicious teatime treat.

The whole range of berries can be used in these recipes – ring the changes by substituting other berries or currants, or use what's readily available. Whatever you choose, the results will be more than satisfying.

# BLUEBERRY MUFFINS

**MAKES 10–12**

250 g/9 oz plain white flour

1 tsp baking powder

pinch of salt

100 g/3¹/₂ oz demerara sugar, plus 1 tbsp for sprinkling

1 egg, beaten

225 ml/8 fl oz milk

55 g/2 oz unsalted butter, melted

125 g/4¹/₂ oz small fresh blueberries

THESE MUFFINS ARE DELICIOUS SERVED WARM. THEY ARE BEST EATEN ON THE DAY OF BAKING, BECAUSE THEY DO NOT STORE WELL.

Preheat the oven to 180°C/350°F/Gas Mark 4. Line a 12-hole muffin tin with muffin paper cases.

Sieve the flour, baking powder and salt into a large bowl and stir in the sugar.

Add the beaten egg, milk and melted butter to the dry ingredients and stir in lightly until just combined – do not overmix. Carefully fold in the blueberries.

Spoon the mixture into the paper cases, taking care not to overfill, and sprinkle with the remaining sugar.

Bake in the preheated oven for 25–30 minutes until golden brown and firm. Transfer to a wire rack to cool a little.

# LOGANBERRY AND CHOCOLATE BROWNIES

**MAKES 9–12**

175 g/6 oz unsalted butter, plus extra for greasing

175 g/6 oz plain chocolate, broken into pieces

225 g/8 oz golden caster sugar

pinch of salt

3 large eggs, beaten

115 g/4 oz plain flour

175 g/6 oz fresh loganberries

Preheat the oven to 180°C/350°F/Gas Mark 4. Grease and line a 20-cm/8-inch square cake tin with non-stick baking paper.

Put the butter and chocolate in a large, heatproof bowl, set the bowl over a saucepan of barely simmering water and heat until melted. Stir until smooth, remove from the heat and leave to cool slightly.

Stir the sugar and salt into the chocolate mixture, then gradually beat in the eggs.

Sieve the flour into the mixture and beat until smooth. Carefully stir in the loganberries.

Scrape the mixture into the prepared tin and bake in the preheated oven for 25–30 minutes, until the top is a pale brown but the middle is dense and gooey.

Remove from the oven and leave to cool in the tin slightly before cutting into squares (cut to the size you prefer).

Leave to cool completely before removing from the tin. Peel off the lining paper.

THESE BROWNIES CAN BE SERVED WITH ICE CREAM AND SOME LOGANBERRY SAUCE FOR A DELICIOUS DESSERT.

# STRAWBERRY SHORTCAKE

**SERVES 8**

175 g/6 oz self-raising flour

100 g/3¹/₂ oz unsalted butter, diced and chilled, plus extra for greasing

75 g/2³/₄ oz caster sugar

1 egg yolk

1 tbsp rosewater

600 ml/1 pint whipping cream, lightly whipped

225 g/8 oz strawberries, hulled and quartered, plus a few whole strawberries, to decorate

*To decorate*

fresh strawberry leaf or mint leaves

icing sugar

Preheat the oven to 190°C/375°F/Gas Mark 5. Lightly grease 2 baking sheets.

To make the shortcakes, sieve the flour into a bowl. Rub in the butter with your fingers until the mixture resembles breadcrumbs. Stir in the sugar, then add the egg yolk and rosewater and mix to form a soft dough.

THE SHORTCAKE CAN BE MADE A FEW DAYS IN ADVANCE AND STORED IN AN AIRTIGHT CONTAINER UNTIL REQUIRED.

Divide the dough in half. Roll out each piece into a 19-cm/7¹/₂-inch round and transfer each one to a prepared baking sheet. Crimp the edges of the dough.

Bake in the preheated oven for 15 minutes until lightly golden. Transfer the shortcakes to a wire rack to cool.

Mix the cream with the strawberry quarters and spoon on top of one of the shortcakes. Top with the other shortcake round, decorate with whole strawberries and a strawberry leaf or mint leaves, and dust with a little icing sugar.

# FRUITY FLAPJACKS

**MAKES 18**

225 g/8 oz unsalted butter, plus extra for greasing

200 g/7 oz light muscovado sugar

85 g/3 oz golden syrup

450 g/1 lb porridge oats

2 tsp ground cinnamon

115 g/4 oz dried berries (cranberries and blueberries are often sold together)

Preheat the oven to 180°C/350°F/Gas Mark 4. Line a 20 × 30-cm/8 × 12-inch deep baking tin with non-stick baking paper.

Put the butter, sugar and syrup in a saucepan and heat over a low heat until melted.

Add the porridge oats and cinnamon and stir well. Add the dried berries and stir to distribute them evenly throughout the oats.

Pour the mixture into the prepared baking tin, press down well and bake in the centre of the preheated oven for 30–35 minutes, until golden-brown but still moist and slightly soft when pressed.

Remove from the oven and leave to cool for 5 minutes. Cut into 18 pieces and leave to cool completely before removing from the tin.

THESE FLAPJACKS CAN BE STORED IN AN AIRTIGHT CONTAINER FOR UP TO 3–4 DAYS. HONEY CAN BE USED IN PLACE OF THE GOLDEN SYRUP FOR A SLIGHTLY LESS SWEET VERSION.

# SUMMER FRUIT TARTLETS

**MAKES 12**

*Pastry*

200 g/7 oz plain flour, plus extra for dusting

85 g/3 oz icing sugar

55 g/2 oz ground almonds

115 g/4 oz unsalted butter, diced and chilled

1 egg yolk

1 tbsp milk

*Filling*

275 g/9¾ oz unsalted cream cheese

icing sugar, to taste, plus extra for dusting

350 g/12 oz fresh summer berries and currants, such as blueberries, raspberries, small strawberries, redcurrants and whitecurrants, picked over and prepared

To make the pastry, sift the flour and sugar into a bowl, then stir in the almonds. Rub in the butter with your fingertips until the mixture resembles breadcrumbs. Add the egg yolk and milk and mix to form a dough. Turn out on to a lightly floured surface and knead briefly. Wrap and chill in the refrigerator for 30 minutes.

Preheat the oven to 200°C/400°F/Gas Mark 6. Roll out the pastry and use it to line 12 deep tartlet or individual brioche tins. Prick the pastry bases with a fork. Press a piece of foil into each tartlet, covering the edges, and bake in the preheated oven for 10–15 minutes, or until light golden-brown. Remove the foil and bake for a further 2–3 minutes. Transfer the pastry cases to a wire rack to cool.

To make the filling, mix the cream cheese and sugar together in a bowl. Put a spoonful of filling in each pastry case and arrange the fruit on top. Dust with sifted icing sugar and serve immediately.

IF YOU WASH THE SUMMER FRUIT JUST BEFORE USING IT, BE SURE TO DRAIN WELL ON KITCHEN PAPER, OTHERWISE THE LIQUID WILL MAKE THE PASTRY CASES SOGGY.

# FOREST FRUIT PIE

**SERVES 4**

*Filling*

250 g/9 oz fresh
blueberries

250 g/9 oz fresh
raspberries

250 g/9 oz fresh
blackberries

100 g/3¹/2 oz caster sugar

2 tbsp icing sugar, to
decorate

whipped cream, to serve

*Pastry*

200 g/7 oz plain flour, plus
extra for dusting

25 g/1 oz ground
hazelnuts

100 g/3¹/2 oz unsalted
butter, diced and chilled,
plus extra for greasing

finely grated rind of
1 lemon

1 egg yolk, beaten

4 tbsp milk

Pick over the berries and put in a saucepan with 3 tablespoons of the caster sugar and cook over a medium heat, stirring frequently, for 5 minutes. Remove from the heat.

To make the pastry, sieve the flour into a bowl, then stir in the hazelnuts. Rub in the butter with your fingertips until the mixture resembles breadcrumbs, then sieve in the remaining caster sugar. Add the lemon rind, egg yolk and 3 tablespoons of the milk and mix to form a dough. Turn out on to a lightly floured work surface and knead briefly. Wrap with clingfilm and chill in the refrigerator for 30 minutes.

Preheat the oven to 190°C/375°F/Gas Mark 5. Grease a 20-cm/8-inch pie dish with butter. Roll out two-thirds of the pastry to a thickness of 5 mm/¹/4 inch and use it to line the base and side of the dish. Spoon the berries into the pastry case. Brush the rim with water, then roll out the remaining pastry and use it to cover the pie. Trim and crimp round the edge, then make 2 small slits in the top and decorate with 2 leaf shapes cut out from the dough trimmings. Brush all over with the remaining milk. Bake in the preheated oven for 40 minutes.

Dust the pie with the icing sugar and serve with whipped cream.

YOU COULD USE OTHER KINDS OF BERRIES IN THIS PIE, SUCH AS LOGANBERRIES OR BILBERRIES. GROUND HAZELNUTS AND LEMON RIND ARE ADDED TO THE PASTRY FOR EXTRA FLAVOUR, BUT YOU COULD SUBSTITUTE GROUND PISTACHIO NUTS AND LIME RIND FOR AN ALTERNATIVE TASTE.

# BRAMBLE TART WITH CASSIS CREAM

**SERVES 6**

*Pastry*

350 g/12 oz plain flour, plus extra for dusting

pinch of salt

175 g/6 oz unsalted butter, diced and chilled

50 g/1³/4 oz caster sugar

5 tsp semolina

1 egg white

*Filling*

750 g/1 lb 10 oz fresh blackberries

6 tbsp golden caster sugar

1 tbsp crème de cassis

*Cassis cream*

250 ml/9 fl oz double cream

1 tbsp crème de cassis

To make the pastry, sieve the flour and salt into a large bowl and rub in the butter with your fingertips until the mixture resembles breadcrumbs. Stir in the caster sugar and add enough cold water to form a dough. Turn out on to a lightly floured work surface and knead briefly. Wrap with clingfilm and chill in the refrigerator for 30 minutes.

Meanwhile, pick over the blackberries, put in a bowl with 4 tablespoons of the golden caster sugar and the cassis and stir to coat. Preheat the oven to 200°C/400°F/Gas Mark 6.

Roll out the pastry into a large circle, handling carefully because it is quite a soft dough. Leave the edges ragged and place on a baking sheet. Sprinkle the pastry with the semolina, leaving a good 6-cm/2¹/2-inch margin around the edge. Pile the fruit into the middle and brush the edges of the pastry with some of the egg white. Fold in the edge of the pastry to overlap and enclose the fruit, making sure to press the pastry together in order to close any gaps. Brush with the remaining egg white, sprinkle with the

remaining sugar and bake in the preheated oven for 25 minutes.

Meanwhile, to make the Cassis Cream, whip the cream in a bowl until it begins to thicken, then stir in the cassis.

Serve the tart hot, straight from the oven, with a good dollop of the Cassis Cream.

THIS TART CAN ALSO BE MADE WITH A MIXTURE OF BERRIES AND FRUIT – MIX SOME RASPBERRIES, SLICED STRAWBERRIES OR SLICES OF RIPE PLUM OR PEACH IN WITH THE BLACKBERRIES. USE A NON-ALCOHOLIC BLACKBERRY-FLAVOURED CORDIAL IN PLACE OF THE CASSIS. THIS TART IS ALSO GOOD SERVED WITH ICE CREAM.

# FRUIT COBBLER

**SERVES 6**

900 g/2 lb fresh berries
and currants, such as
blackberries, blueberries,
raspberries, redcurrants
and blackcurrants

85–115 g/3–4 oz caster
sugar

2 tbsp cornflour

*Cobbler topping*

200 g/7 oz plain flour

2 tsp baking powder

pinch of salt

55 g/2 oz unsalted butter,
diced and chilled

2 tbsp caster sugar

175 ml/6 fl oz buttermilk

1 tbsp demerara sugar

single or double cream,
to serve

Preheat the oven to 200°C/400°F/Gas Mark 6.
Pick over the fruit, mix with the caster sugar and
cornflour and put in a 25-cm/10-inch shallow,
ovenproof dish.

To make the topping, sieve the flour, baking
powder and salt into a large bowl. Rub in the
butter until the mixture resembles breadcrumbs,
then stir in the caster sugar. Pour in the
buttermilk and mix to a soft dough.

Drop spoonfuls of the dough on top of the
fruit roughly, so that it doesn't completely cover
the fruit. Sprinkle with the demerara sugar and
bake in the preheated oven for 25–30 minutes
until the crust is golden and the fruit is tender.

Remove from the oven and leave to stand for
a few minutes before serving with cream.

INSTEAD OF BUTTERMILK, YOU CAN USE MILK WITH
A GOOD SQUEEZE OF LIME JUICE ADDED.

# APPLE AND BLACKBERRY CRUMBLE

**SERVES 4**

900 g/2 lb cooking apples

300 g/10¹/₂ oz blackberries, fresh or frozen

55 g/2 oz light muscovado sugar

1 tsp ground cinnamon

custard or pouring cream, to serve

*Crumble*

85 g/3 oz self-raising flour

85 g/3 oz wholemeal plain flour

115 g/4 oz unsalted butter

55 g/2 oz demerara sugar

WHEN MAKING A CRUMBLE, KEEP RUBBING IN THE BUTTER UNTIL THE CRUMBS ARE QUITE COARSE. THIS ENSURES THAT THE CRUMBLE WILL BE CRUNCHY.

Preheat the oven to 200°C/400°F/Gas Mark 6. Peel and core the apples, then cut into chunks. Put in a bowl with the blackberries, muscovado sugar and cinnamon and mix together, then transfer to an ovenproof baking dish.

To make the crumble, sieve the self-raising flour into a bowl and stir in the wholemeal flour. Rub in the butter with your fingertips until the mixture resembles coarse breadcrumbs. Stir in the demerara sugar.

Spread the crumble over the apples and bake in the preheated oven for 40–45 minutes, or until the apples are soft and the crumble is golden brown and crisp. Serve with custard or pouring cream.

# RASPBERRY
# DESSERT CAKE

**SERVES 8–10**

250 g/9 oz plain
chocolate, broken into
pieces

225 g/8 oz unsalted
butter, plus extra
for greasing

1 tbsp strong, dark coffee

5 eggs

100 g/3 1/2 oz golden
caster sugar

85 g/3 oz plain flour

1 tsp ground cinnamon

175 g/6 oz fresh
raspberries, plus extra
to serve

icing sugar, for dusting

whipped cream, to serve

Preheat the oven to 160°C/325°F/Gas Mark 3.
Grease a 23-cm/9-inch cake tin and line the base
with non-stick baking paper. Put the chocolate,
butter and coffee in a small, heatproof bowl, set
the bowl over a saucepan of barely simmering
water and heat until melted. Remove from the
heat, stir and leave to cool slightly.

Beat the eggs and caster sugar together in a
separate bowl until pale and thick. Gently fold in
the chocolate mixture.

Sift the flour and cinnamon into another bowl,
then fold into the chocolate mixture. Pour into
the prepared tin and sprinkle the raspberries
evenly over the top.

Bake in the preheated oven for about 35–45
minutes, or until the cake is well risen and
springy to the touch. Leave to cool in the tin
for 15 minutes before turning out on to a large
serving plate. Dust with icing sugar before
serving with extra fresh raspberries and
whipped cream.

IF FRESH RASPBERRIES ARE NOT AVAILABLE,
FROZEN RASPBERRIES MAY BE USED. SINCE
THESE WILL BE SOFTER THAN FRESH FRUIT,
TAKE CARE TO THAW THEM THOROUGHLY
AND DRAIN OFF ANY EXCESS JUICE.

# GOOSEBERRY CHEESECAKE

**SERVES 8**

*Base*

4 tbsp unsalted butter

225 g/8 oz digestive biscuits, crushed

55 g/2 oz chopped walnuts

*Filling*

450 g/1 lb mascarpone cheese

2 eggs, beaten

100 g/3½ oz caster sugar

250 g/9 oz white chocolate, broken into pieces

250 g/9 oz gooseberries

*Topping*

175 g/6 oz mascarpone cheese

white and plain chocolate curls

16 whole strawberries

Preheat the oven to 150°C/300°F/Gas Mark 2. To make the base, melt the butter in a saucepan over a low heat and stir in the crushed biscuits and nuts. Spoon the mixture into a 23-cm/9-inch loose-based cake tin and press evenly over the base with the back of a spoon. Set aside.

To make the filling, beat the cheese in a bowl until smooth, then beat in the eggs and 3 tablespoons of the sugar.

Put the chocolate in the top of a double boiler over a low heat or in a heatproof bowl set over a saucepan of barely simmering water and stir until melted and smooth. Remove from the heat and leave to cool slightly.

Put the gooseberries and remaining sugar in a saucepan and heat over a low heat, stirring, until the sugar has dissolved. Cook gently for 1–2 minutes until the gooseberries are softened but still whole. Leave to cool.

Add the cooled chocolate and gooseberries to the filling. Spoon the mixture over the biscuit base, spread out evenly and smooth the surface. Bake in the preheated oven for 1 hour, or until the filling is just firm. Turn off the oven, but leave the cheesecake in the oven until it is completely cold.

Transfer the cheesecake to a serving plate and spread the mascarpone cheese on top. Decorate with chocolate curls and whole strawberries.

YOU CAN MAKE CHOCOLATE CURLS QUICKLY AND EASILY BY RUNNING A SWIVEL-BLADED VEGETABLE PEELER DOWN THE SIDE OF A CHUNKY BAR OF CHOCOLATE.

Desserts are where berries really come into their own. We all love the simple pleasure of eating freshly picked summer berries just as they come, but they can be enjoyed in many different creative ways that take very little time and effort. For instance, the addition of some whipped cream and a little sugar swirled into a berry purée makes a delectable, eye-catching fruit fool. What could be easier than dipping berries into melted dark chocolate, either to be eaten immediately fondue-style, or leaving the chocolate to harden to serve as petits fours at the end of a meal. A mixture of different chocolate-dipped berries, with their jewel-like colours and pleasing shapes and textures, makes a great centrepiece for a dinner party.

# PART FOUR
# THE PERFECT FINALE

But sometimes something more extravagant is called for to provide a fitting finale to a special-occasion meal. A soufflé never fails to provide the wow factor, and the recipe here features an imaginative combination of cranberries and orange. Trifles are another success story, and here we have raspberries and strawberries laced with a berry liqueur and topped with a sumptuous authentic custard.

As the season progresses, berries tend to become larger and softer, and this plump quality makes them ideal for cooking. The resulting purées make delicious ice-cold berry sorbets – wonderfully refreshing for a hot day or a balmy summer's evening.

# CRANBERRY AND ORANGE SOUFFLÉ

**SERVES 4–6**

400 g/14 oz cranberries, fresh or frozen

150 ml/5 fl oz water

175 g/6 oz caster sugar

grated rind of 2 oranges

3 eggs, separated

15 g/½ oz powdered gelatine

3 tbsp orange juice

150 ml/5 fl oz double cream, whipped until soft and thick

55 g/2 oz finely chopped almonds, toasted

150 ml/5 fl oz single cream, to serve (optional)

orange zest, to decorate

First make the cranberry purée. Put the cranberries, water and 55 g/2 oz of the sugar in a saucepan and cook over a low heat for 2–3 minutes, until the sugar has dissolved and the berries have formed a rich syrup. Leave to cool. Using the back of a wooden spoon, press through a nylon sieve into a bowl to form a purée. You should get about 300 ml/10 fl oz. Stir in the orange rind.

Whisk the egg yolks and remaining sugar with an electric mixer until thick and light.

Put the gelatine in a heatproof cup with the orange juice and soak for 1–2 minutes until it is spongy. Put the cup in a small saucepan with enough water to come halfway up the sides and heat over a low heat for 2–3 minutes, until the gelatine has dissolved and the mixture is clear. Leave to cool until it is the same temperature as the fruit purée, then stir into the fruit purée.

Fold the fruit purée evenly into the egg mixture and then fold in the whipped cream.

Whisk the egg whites in a grease-free bowl until stiff but not too dry and then fold gently into the mixture.

Pour the mixture into a glass serving dish and smooth the top with a palette knife. Chill in the refrigerator for 3–4 hours until firm.

Decorate with the nuts and orange zest and serve with a little cream poured over the top, if using.

To make a proper soufflé, use a 15-cm/6-inch soufflé dish and tie a double layer of baking paper around the outside with string. The paper should stand up above the rim of the dish by 3 cm/1¼ inches. Brush the inside of the paper with oil. Once chilled, carefully remove the paper collar and gently press the nuts on to the side of the soufflé.

# CHOCOLATE PANCAKES WITH BERRY COMPOTE

**MAKES 8-10**

115 g/4 oz plain flour

25 g/1 oz cocoa powder

pinch of salt

1 egg

25 g/1 oz caster sugar

350 ml/12 fl oz milk

50 g/1¾ oz butter

icing sugar, for dusting

ice cream or pouring cream, to serve

*Berry compote*

150 g/5½ oz fresh blackberries

150 g/5½ oz fresh blueberries

225 g/8 oz fresh raspberries

55 g/2 oz caster sugar

juice of ½ lemon

½ tsp mixed spice (optional)

Preheat the oven to 140°C/275°F/Gas Mark 1. Sift the flour, cocoa powder and salt together into a large bowl and make a well in the centre.

Beat the egg, sugar and half the milk together in a separate bowl, then pour the mixture into the dry ingredients. Beat the dry ingredients into the liquid, gradually drawing them in from the side, until a smooth batter is formed. Gradually beat in the remaining milk. Pour the batter into a jug.

Heat an 18-cm/7-inch non-stick frying pan over a medium heat and add 1 teaspoon of the butter.

When the butter has melted, pour in enough batter just to cover the base, then swirl it round the pan while tilting it so that you have a thin,

even layer. Cook for 30 seconds and then lift up the edge of the pancake to check if it is cooked. Loosen the pancake around the edge, then flip it over with a spatula or palette knife. Alternatively, toss the pancake by flipping the frying pan quickly with a flick of the wrist and catching it carefully. Cook on the other side until the base is golden brown.

Transfer the pancake to a warmed plate and keep warm in the preheated oven while you cook the remaining batter, adding the remaining butter to the frying pan as necessary. Make a stack of the pancakes with baking paper in between each pancake.

To make the compote, pick over the berries and put in a saucepan with the sugar, lemon juice and mixed spice, if using. Cook over a low heat until the sugar has dissolved and the berries are warmed through. Do not overcook.

Put a pancake on a warmed serving plate and spoon some of the compote on to the centre. Either roll or fold the pancake and dust with icing sugar. Repeat with the remaining pancakes. Serve with ice cream or pouring cream.

FOR A MORE INDULGENT DESSERT, SERVE WITH HOT CHOCOLATE SAUCE MADE BY MELTING 115 G/4 OZ PLAIN CHOCOLATE WITH 125 ML/4 FL OZ DOUBLE CREAM.

# BLUEBERRY ROULADE

**SERVES 8**

3 large eggs

125 g/4¹/₂ oz caster sugar

125 g/4¹/₂ oz plain flour

1 tbsp hot water

15 g/¹/₂ oz flaked almonds, toasted

1 tsp icing sugar

*Filling*

200 ml/7 fl oz low-fat fromage frais

1 tsp almond essence

150 g/5¹/₂ oz small fresh blueberries

1 tbsp caster sugar

Preheat the oven to 220°C/425°F/Gas Mark 7. Line a 35 x 25-cm/14 x 10-inch Swiss roll tin with non-stick baking paper. Put the eggs in a large, heatproof bowl with the caster sugar, set over a saucepan of hot water and, using an electric whisk, whisk until pale and thick.

Remove the bowl from the saucepan. Sieve the flour, then fold into the egg mixture with the hot water. Pour the mixture into the prepared tin and bake in the preheated oven for 8–10 minutes, or until golden and set.

Transfer the sponge to a sheet of non-stick baking paper. Peel off the lining paper and roll up the sponge tightly along with the baking paper. Wrap in a clean tea towel and leave to cool.

Meanwhile, to make the filling, mix the fromage frais and almond essence together in a bowl. Reserve a few blueberries for decoration, then put the remainder in a separate bowl and sprinkle with the caster sugar. Cover the fromage frais mixture and the fruit with clingfilm and leave to chill in the refrigerator until required.

Unroll the sponge, spread the fromage frais mixture over the sponge and sprinkle with the blueberries. Roll the sponge up again and transfer to a serving plate. Sprinkle with the almonds and dust with the icing sugar. Decorate with the reserved blueberries and serve.

TO PREVENT THE SPONGE FROM BREAKING WHEN YOU ROLL IT UP WITH THE FILLING IN PLACE, MANIPULATE IT WITH THE BAKING PAPER, NOT YOUR FINGERS, AND WORK SLOWLY AND CAREFULLY.

# CHOCOLATE AND STRAWBERRY BRULEES

**SERVES 6**

250 g/9 oz fresh strawberries, plus extra to decorate

2 tbsp fruit liqueur, such as kirsch or crème de cassis

450 ml/16 fl oz double cream

115 g/4 oz plain chocolate, melted and cooled

115 g/4 oz demerara sugar

fresh mint leaves, to decorate

Pick over the strawberries and hull. Cut into halves or quarters, depending on their size, and divide between 6 ramekin dishes. Sprinkle over the fruit liqueur.

Pour the cream into a bowl and whip until it is just holding its shape. Add the cooled chocolate and continue whipping until the cream is thick. Spread over the strawberries. Cover and freeze for 2 hours, or until the cream is frozen.

Preheat the grill to high. Sprinkle the sugar thickly over the cream, then cook under the grill until the sugar has melted and caramelized.

Leave the brûlées to stand for 30 minutes, or until the fruit and cream have thawed. Serve decorated with a few extra strawberries and some mint leaves.

FREEZING THE BRULEES BEFORE GRILLING ENSURES THAT THE CREAM WILL NOT BUBBLE UP THROUGH THE SUGAR, HOWEVER, IF YOU ARE SHORT OF TIME, IT IS NOT NECESSARY TO FREEZE THEM. YOU CAN CARAMELIZE THE SUGAR WITH A CULINARY BLOWTORCH.

# CHOCOLATE-DIPPED FRUIT

**SERVES 4**

12 physalis (Cape gooseberries)

200 g/7 oz plain chocolate, broken into pieces

1 tbsp sunflower oil

12 small strawberries

Line a baking sheet with non-stick baking paper. Peel back the papery outer case from the physalis and twist at the top to make a 'handle'.

Put the chocolate and oil in a small, heatproof bowl, set the bowl over a saucepan of barely simmering water and heat until the chocolate has melted. Remove from the heat, stir and leave to cool until tepid.

Dip the fruit in the chocolate mixture and let any excess drain back into the saucepan. The fruit does not need to be completely coated.

Set the fruit on the prepared baking sheet. If the chocolate forms a 'foot' on the paper, it is too warm, so leave to cool slightly. If the chocolate in the bowl begins to set, warm it gently over the saucepan of simmering water. Chill the dipped fruit in the refrigerator for 30 minutes, or until the chocolate is set, then peel away from the paper. Serve on their own, or use to decorate another dessert.

LARGE CHERRIES WOULD MAKE A GOOD ALTERNATIVE OR ADDITION TO THE STRAWBERRIES AND CAPE GOOSEBERRIES.

# BLUEBERRY JELLY
## WITH CASSIS

**SERVES 4–6**

450 g/1 lb fresh
blueberries, plus extra
to decorate

150 ml/5 fl oz water

225 g/8 oz caster sugar

175 ml/6 fl oz crème de
cassis

15 g/¹/2 oz powdered
gelatine

3 tbsp water

*To decorate*

fresh mint leaves

icing sugar, sifted, for
dusting

TO MAKE INDIVIDUAL JELLIES, YOU CAN POUR
THE FRUIT MIXTURE INTO INDIVIDUAL GLASSES
OR DISHES AND FLOAT THE CREAM ON TOP
BEFORE SERVING.

Put the blueberries, water and sugar in a saucepan and cook over a medium heat until softened.

Remove from the heat and leave to cool. Crush the berries with a wooden spoon to make a smooth purée.

Pour the purée into a measuring jug and add the cassis. Make up to 600 ml/1 pint, adding extra water if necessary.

Put the gelatine and the water in a heatproof cup and soak for 1–2 minutes until it is spongy. Put the cup in a small saucepan with enough water to come halfway up the sides, and heat over a low heat for 2–3 minutes until the gelatine has dissolved and the mixture is clear. Leave to cool until it is the same temperature as the fruit purée.

Mix the blueberry mixture and the gelatine together and pour into a jelly mould or a glass serving bowl. Cover with clingfilm and chill in the refrigerator until set. Decorate with fresh blueberries and mint leaves, dust with sifted icing sugar and serve.

# BERRY TRIFLE

**SERVES 6–8**

8 trifle sponges

100 g/3¹/₂ oz raspberry
jam

150 ml/5 fl oz crème de
cassis or framboise

225 g/8 oz fresh
raspberries

225 g/8 oz fresh
strawberries

*Custard*

425 ml/15 fl oz single
cream

5 egg yolks

3 tbsp caster sugar

¹/₂ tsp vanilla extract

*Topping*

300 ml/10 fl oz double
cream

2 tbsp milk

40 g/1¹/₂ oz toasted flaked
almonds

Break the trifle sponges into pieces and spread
with the jam. Put in a glass serving bowl and
pour over the fruit liqueur. Pick over the
berries and hull if necessary. Spoon on top
of the sponge.

To make the custard, heat the single cream in
a small saucepan until just coming up to boiling
point. Using a wooden spoon, beat the egg yolks,
sugar and vanilla extract together in a heatproof
measuring jug. Pour the hot cream into the jug,
stirring constantly, until well mixed. Return the
mixture to the rinsed-out saucepan and heat
very gently, stirring constantly, over the lowest
heat until the sauce has thickened enough
to coat the back of the wooden spoon.
Immediately put the base of the saucepan in
a bowl of cold water to prevent it overcooking.
Stir until cooled.

Pour the custard over the trifle base, cover
with clingfilm and leave to settle in the
refrigerator for 2–3 hours or overnight.

Just before serving, whip the double cream
with the milk in a bowl until thick but still soft.
Spoon over the custard and swirl around using a
knife to give an attractive appearance. Decorate
with the toasted almonds, cover with clingfilm
and chill in the refrigerator before serving.

IF YOU PREFER, YOU CAN MAKE
THE TRIFLE IN INDIVIDUAL
SERVING DISHES INSTEAD.

# GOOSEBERRY FOOL

**SERVES 6**

700 g/1 lb 9 oz fresh
gooseberries

115 g/4 oz caster sugar

3 tbsp elderflower cordial

300 ml/10 fl oz double
cream

lemon balm or mint
leaves, to decorate

crisp biscuits or sponge
fingers, to serve

Top and tail the gooseberries and put in a saucepan with the sugar. Cook over a low heat, stirring constantly, until the fruit is softened to a pulp.

Remove from the heat and beat well with a wooden spoon until you have a thick purée. If you would like a smoother consistency, use the back of a wooden spoon to press the purée through a nylon sieve into a bowl to remove the seeds. Stir in the elderflower cordial. Taste for sweetness at this point and add a little more sugar if needed. Leave to cool.

Whip the cream in a bowl until it is thick but not too dry. Using a metal spoon, gently fold in the cold gooseberry purée until only just combined – the fool looks more attractive if it has a marbled appearance.

Spoon into 6 glass serving dishes or 1 large glass bowl, cover with clingfilm and chill well in the refrigerator. Decorate with lemon balm or mint leaves and serve with crisp biscuits or sponge fingers.

# RED BERRY SORBET

**SERVES 6**

225 g/8 oz fresh redcurrants, plus extra to decorate

225 g/8 oz fresh raspberries, plus extra to decorate

175 ml/6 fl oz water

115 g/4 oz sugar

150 ml/5 fl oz cranberry juice

2 egg whites

fresh mint sprigs, to decorate

Strip the redcurrants from their stalks using the prongs of a fork and put in a large, heavy-based saucepan with the raspberries. Add 30 ml/1 fl oz of the water and cook over a low heat for 10 minutes, or until softened. Using the back of a wooden spoon, press the fruit through a nylon sieve into a bowl to form a purée.

Put the sugar and the remaining water in the rinsed-out saucepan and heat over a low heat, stirring, until the sugar has dissolved. Bring to the boil, then boil, without stirring, for 10 minutes to form a syrup. Do not allow it to brown. Remove from the heat and leave to cool for at least an hour. When cold, stir the fruit purée and cranberry juice into the syrup.

If using an ice cream machine, churn the mixture in the machine following the manufacturer's instructions. When the mixture begins to freeze, whisk the egg whites until they just hold their shape but are not dry, then add to the mixture and continue churning. Alternatively, freeze the mixture in a rigid freezerproof container, uncovered, for 3–4 hours, or until mushy. Turn the mixture into a bowl and stir with a fork or beat in a blender or food processor to break down the ice crystals. Lightly whisk the egg whites until stiff but not dry, then fold them into the mixture. Return to the freezer and freeze for a further 3–4 hours, or until firm or required. Cover the container with a lid for storing. Serve scattered with extra fruit and mint sprigs.

IT IS POSSIBLE TO USE A VARIETY OF SOFT FRUIT IN THIS RECIPE, ALTHOUGH YOU WON'T NECESSARILY END UP WITH A RED BERRY SORBET! CHOOSE FROM STRAWBERRIES, BLACKBERRIES AND BLACKCURRANTS.

# GOOSEBERRY AND ELDERFLOWER SORBET

**SERVES 6**

115 g/4 oz sugar

600 ml/1 pint water

500 g/1 lb 2 oz fresh gooseberries, not topped and tailed, plus extra to serve

125 ml/4 fl oz elderflower cordial

1 tbsp lemon juice

few drops of green food colouring (optional)

125 ml/4 fl oz double cream

ice cream biscuits, to serve

Put the sugar and water in a large, heavy-based saucepan and heat over a low heat, stirring, until the sugar has dissolved. Bring to the boil, then add the gooseberries and simmer, stirring occasionally, for 10 minutes, or until very tender. Remove from the heat and cool for 5 minutes.

Put the gooseberries in a blender or food processor and process until smooth. Using the back of a wooden spoon, press the purée through a nylon sieve into a bowl to remove the seeds. Leave to cool for at least an hour.

Add the elderflower cordial and lemon juice to the gooseberry purée and stir until well mixed. Add the food colouring to tint the mixture pale green, if using. Stir the cream into the mixture.

If using an ice cream machine, churn the mixture in the machine following the manufacturer's instructions. Alternatively, freeze the mixture in a rigid freezerproof container, uncovered, for 3–4 hours, or until mushy. Turn the mixture into a bowl and stir with a fork or beat in a blender or food processor to break down the ice crystals. Return to the freezer and freeze for a further 3–4 hours, or until firm or required. Serve with gooseberries and ice cream biscuits.

WHEN AVAILABLE, INSTEAD OF THE ELDERFLOWER CORDIAL, USE TWO FRESHLY PICKED AND RINSED ELDERFLOWER HEADS, TIED IN A PIECE OF MUSLIN, AND ADD TO THE SAUCEPAN WITH THE GOOSEBERRIES. DISCARD ONCE THE GOOSEBERRIES ARE COOKED.

# HOT BERRY COMPOTE WITH VANILLA ICE CREAM

**SERVES 6**

700 g/1 lb 9 oz summer berries, such as raspberries, blueberries, blackberries and strawberries

175 g/6 oz caster sugar

55 g/2 oz stem ginger in syrup

ice cream biscuits, to serve

*Vanilla ice cream*

450 g/1 lb natural bio yogurt

225 g/8 oz caster sugar

1 vanilla pod

300 ml/10 fl oz double cream

Make the ice cream in advance. Pour the yogurt into a bowl and stir in 55 g/2 oz of the sugar. Cut the vanilla pod in half lengthwise, scrape out all the black seeds and add them to the yogurt.

Discard the pod. Whisk the cream in a separate bowl until thick but still soft, then fold into the yogurt mixture.

If using an ice cream machine, churn the mixture in the machine following the manufacturer's instructions. Alternatively, freeze the mixture in a rigid freezerproof container, covered, for 1 hour. Turn the mixture into a bowl and stir with a fork or beat in a blender or food processor to break

down the ice crystals. Return to the freezer and freeze for a further hour. Repeat until the mixture is completely frozen. Transfer the ice cream to the refrigerator 15 minutes before serving.

Pick over the berries and hull if necessary. Put the fruit in a saucepan with the remaining sugar and heat over a low heat until the sugar until has dissolved and the fruit juices begin to run. Do not overcook. Finely chop the stem ginger and add to the fruit.

Put the ice cream in individual serving dishes, pour over the hot compote and serve immediately with ice cream biscuits.

YOU COULD ALSO USE SOME REDCURRANTS OR BLACKCURRANTS WITH THE BERRIES. THE ICE CREAM CAN BE KEPT IN THE FREEZER FOR UP TO ONE MONTH.

# INDEX